W9-AXG-346

The Montgomery Bus Boycott

The Montgomery Bus Boycott

Dennis Brindell Fradin

mc **Marshall Cavendish**
Benchmark

New York

Marshall Cavendish Benchmark
99 White Plains Road
Tarrytown, NY 10591
www.marshallcavendish.us

Library of Congress Cataloging-in-Publication Data

Fradin, Dennis B.
The Montgomery Bus Boycott / by Dennis Brindell Fradin.
p. cm. — (Turning points in U.S. history)
Includes bibliographical references and index.
Summary: "Covers the Montgomery bus boycott as a watershed event in U.S. history,
influencing social, economic, and political policies that shaped the nation's future"—Provided by publisher.
ISBN 978-0-7614-4258-5
1. Montgomery Bus Boycott, Montgomery, Ala., 1955-1956—Juvenile literature. 2. African Americans—Civil rights—Alabama—
Montgomery—History—20th century—Juvenile literature. 3. Segregation in transportation—Alabama—Montgomery—History—
20th century—Juvenile literature. 4. Civil rights movements—Alabama—Montgomery—History—20th century—Juvenile literature.
5. Montgomery (Ala.)—Race relations—History—20th century—Juvenile literature. I. Title.
F334.M79N429 2009
323.1196'073076147—dc22
2008036007

Photo Research by Connie Gardner
Cover photo by Bettmann/CORBIS
Cover: An interior view of a Montgomery city transit bus, 1956
Title Page: A painted limewood sculpture by Marshall D. Rumbaugh depicts Rosa Parks's arrest.

The photographs in this book are used by permission and through the courtesy of: *AP Photo:* Fred Gay, 22;
Art Resource: National Portrait Gallery, Smithsonian Institution, 3; *Granger Collection:* 6, 10, 13, 14, 17; *Corbis:* Frances Benjamin Johnston, 12;
Bettmann, 16, 25, 28, 34, 36; *Getty Images:* Hank Walker, 18; Time Life Pictures, 26, 30, 32, 42-43; Hulton Archive, 38.

Timeline: Getty Images: Hank Walker

Editor: Deborah Grahame
Publisher: Michelle Bisson
Art Director: Anahid Hamparian
Printed in Malaysia
1 3 5 6 4 2

Contents

Slaves pick cotton on a Southern plantation in this nineteenth-century photograph.

CHAPTER ONE

Slavery in the United States

Between 1607 and 1733, Britain settled or took over thirteen American **colonies**. All thirteen allowed slavery. The colonies broke free from Britain in 1776 and declared that they had formed the United States of America. Four years later, Massachusetts became the first state to outlaw slavery. Other Northern states followed.

By the mid-1800s, slavery had ended in the North. In the South, though, white people still depended on slaves to grow cotton and other crops. By 1860, 4 million black Southerners were slaves—an eighth of the nation's population.

The Civil War between the Northern (Union) and Southern (Confederate) states began in 1861. The issue of slavery was one of the war's main causes.

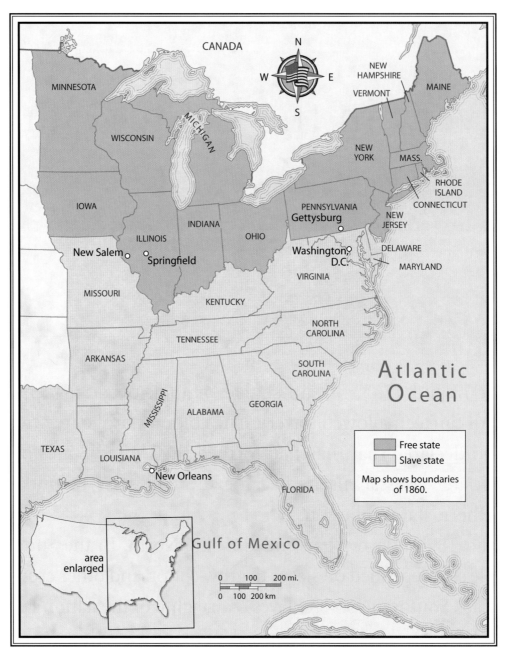

This map depicts free states (blue) and slave states (white) in the 1860s.

The North won the war in 1865. That December, the Thirteenth **Amendment** to the U.S. **Constitution**, which ended slavery in the United States, was passed. In 1868, the Fourteenth Amendment guaranteed African Americans equal rights as citizens.

For a few years after the Civil War, U.S. soldiers remained in the South. They tried to make sure that whites treated newly freed African Americans fairly. During this period, black children began to attend school, which was not allowed in the days of slavery. African Americans voted and won public office. Black citizens were headed toward true equality—or so it seemed.

Black pupils are shown being instructed at the Freedman's School in Charleston, South Carolina, in 1866.

CHAPTER TWO

Slavery Ends but Jim Crow Begins

By the late 1870s, the U.S. troops had withdrawn from the South. White Southerners found new ways to mistreat African Americans. **Segregation**—the practice of keeping the races apart—took root in the South. Segregation became known as "Jim Crow," after a song-and-dance routine that made fun of African Americans. Jim Crow laws and **customs** were designed to keep black Southerners from exercising their rights.

Black children in the South had to attend separate schools. The "Negro schools" often lacked books and supplies. African Americans had to ride in separate "Negro cars" on trains. When they got sick, they were treated at poorly equipped "Negro hospitals." In public places, African Americans had to use

African-American students attend an art class in a public school in Washington, D.C., 1899.

Beyond Belief

Many Jim Crow laws and customs were not only hurtful, but also ridiculous. For example, Florida and North Carolina passed laws stating that textbooks used by black and white children could not be stored together.

separate bathrooms and drinking fountains. They were excluded from "Whites-only" hotels, restaurants, parks, swimming pools, and theaters. Black Southerners were also kept from voting and serving on juries.

The Jim Crow practices violated constitutional amendments protecting black people's rights. Yet the federal government did little about it. Northern lawmakers did not want to stir up more trouble with white Southerners. Also, Northerners practiced racial **discrimination** of their own.

To make things worse, the Ku Klux Klan and other hate groups terrorized black people who defied the Jim Crow laws and customs. African

Near Atlanta, Georgia, in 1921, a Ku Klux Klan leader presides over an outdoor meeting.

Americans who entered "Whites-only" bathrooms or parks risked being beaten or killed. Sadly, the U.S. government did little to stop this horrible—and illegal—behavior.

Ida B. Wells (1862–1931) was a teacher, journalist, and early crusader for civil rights.

CHAPTER THREE

Early Struggles against Jim Crow

Many Americans knew that racial discrimination was wrong. Some of them fought Jim Crow practices. And some of them succeeded.

In 1884, Ida B. Wells, a twenty-one-year-old teacher, was riding a train to her school in Woodstock, Tennessee. Three years earlier, Tennessee had made it illegal for black passengers to occupy the same train car as white passengers. Miss Wells thought the law was **immoral**, so she ignored it. She was reading a book in the "White ladies' coach" when the conductor ordered her to the "Negro car." She refused to move and fought the conductor as he tried to drag her from her seat. It took three white men to remove her from the "White ladies' coach."

Jackie Robinson signs autographs for fans before a 1947 Brooklyn Dodgers game.

Miss Wells sued the train company, but she lost her case in the Tennessee Supreme Court. If she had won, the case might have stopped the spread of Jim Crow laws in the South.

Progress came slowly. Not until 1947 did Jackie Robinson break baseball's color barrier. When he joined the Brooklyn Dodgers in that year, he was the first African American to play Major League Baseball.

Another battle against segregation happened soon after. Like other Southern cities, Washington, D.C., excluded black people from its many "Whites-only" restaurants. This was especially shameful because Washington was the nation's capital. How could the United States end discrimination if its capital city would not allow black citizens to eat alongside whites?

D.C. in the South?

Many people do not think of Washington, D.C., as a Southern city, but it is. The land on which the nation's capital city stands came from Maryland, which is a Southern state.

Mary Church Terrell (1863–1954)

Mary Church Terrell gathered a group of black and white people to oppose the capital city's restaurant policy. After a long struggle, Terrell's forces won. In 1953 the U.S. Supreme Court ruled that all of Washington's restaurants must serve black customers.

Another victory came the next year. In 1954, as a result of the *Brown v. Board of Education* case, the nation's highest court ruled that racial segregation in public schools must end.

In compliance with segregations laws, African Americans sit in the back of a bus in this 1950s photograph.

CHAPTER FOUR

Rosa Parks and Bus 2857

Despite some triumphs over discrimination, Jim Crow still ruled in the 1950s. Montgomery, Alabama, was among the hundreds of Southern communities where segregation was standard practice. One form of discrimination in Montgomery involved the city's buses.

The front seats on the buses were reserved for white people. Black Montgomerians were required to sit in the back seats. Even if a bus contained no white passengers, African Americans were not allowed to sit in the "Whites-only" front section. What if white people boarded a bus in which every seat was taken? Then the black passengers had to give up their seats to the white newcomers and stand in the aisle.

A Fertile City

Founded in 1819, Montgomery has been Alabama's capital since 1846. Montgomery is called the Cradle of the Confederacy because Southern leaders formed the Confederate States of America there in 1861.

By 1955, Montgomery had a population of 200,000, about a quarter of whom were African Americans. At that time Montgomery was one of the country's most segregated cities. Because of the bus boycott, Montgomery is sometimes called the birthplace of the civil rights movement.

Now and then citizens challenged the Jim Crow bus arrangement. On March 2, 1955, fifteen-year-old Claudette Colvin was sitting in the "Negro section" of a Montgomery bus. The vehicle was crowded, and a number of black and white people were standing in the aisle. Suddenly, the driver stopped the bus. He ordered black passengers to give up their seats to the whites who were standing.

Some people obeyed, but Colvin would not budge. The driver called for two policemen. Colvin was dragged, kicking and screaming, off the bus. She was handcuffed and briefly jailed.

Black Montgomerians were outraged that a high-school girl could be put in jail for sitting on a bus. African Americans talked about challenging the Jim Crow seating policy. However, it did not happen—yet.

A few months later, on October 21, eighteen-year-old Mary Louise Smith refused to give up her seat on a Montgomery bus. She, too, was arrested.

The event that would bring change occurred on December 1, 1955. Early that Thursday evening, forty-two-year-old Rosa Parks boarded Montgomery bus number 2857. Mrs. Parks had worked a long day at a department store and then had gone Christmas shopping. Carrying her packages, she paid her dime and then sat down in the bus's "Negro section."

When a number of white people boarded the crowded bus, the driver told Mrs. Parks to vacate her seat, but she refused.

"Are you going to stand up?" the driver asked angrily.

"No!" Rosa Parks declared.

"Well, I'm going to have you arrested!" the driver threatened.

"You may do that!" Mrs. Parks told him.

Rosa Parks was arrested and taken to jail. That night Mr. Edgar D. Nixon, a **civil rights** leader in Montgomery, and attorney Clifford Durr bailed her out. Mrs. Parks's trial was scheduled for Monday, December 5.

Jim Crow Bus Code

Montgomery's law regarding bus seating was called Separation of Races Required. It stated, "Every person operating a bus line in the city shall . . . separate the white people from the negroes." A related law gave bus drivers the "powers of a police officer" when telling passengers where to sit. Furthermore, it was "unlawful for any passenger to refuse or fail to take a seat among those assigned to the race to which he belongs."

Rosa Parks appears in court with Edgar D. Nixon (center) and her attorney Fred Gray (right) a few days after her arrest for refusing to give up her seat on the bus.

CHAPTER FIVE

"The Day of Days"

Rosa Parks's arrest was the last straw for thousands of black Montgomerians. They included many members of the Women's Political Council (WPC), a civil rights organization for black women. Upon hearing of Mrs. Parks's arrest, WPC president Jo Ann Robinson planned a one-day **boycott** of Montgomery's buses to protest segregation on the vehicles. Mrs. Robinson wrote the following leaflet:

Another Negro woman has been arrested and thrown in jail because she refused to get up out of her seat on the bus for a white person to sit down. If we do not stop these arrests, they will continue. We are asking every

Negro to stay off the buses Monday in protest of the arrest and trial. Don't ride the bus to work, to town, to school, or anywhere on Monday. If you work, take a cab or walk. But please, children and grown-ups, don't ride the bus at all on Monday.

With the help of two college students, Mrs. Robinson worked all night to print thousands of the leaflets. On Friday, December 2, the WPC passed out the leaflets in African-American neighborhoods. That Sunday, preachers at black churches asked their congregations not to ride the city's buses the next day.

On Monday, December 5, very few black Montgomerians boarded the buses. Instead, they walked or took taxis as Mrs. Robinson had requested. Thanks to Jo Ann Robinson and the WPC, the Montgomery Bus Boycott was underway.

Martin Luther King Jr. later called December 5, 1955, the Day of Days because of all that happened on that Monday. Besides marking the start of the bus boycott, it was the day of Rosa Parks's trial. The judge found Mrs. Parks guilty of disobeying Montgomery's Jim Crow laws. She was fined ten dollars. The money was not a major concern. Instead, the black community was concerned that the judge had upheld the city's right to practice segregation on its buses.

A Woman of Quiet Strength

Rosa Parks (1913–2005) was born in Tuskegee, Alabama. As a child growing up near Montgomery, she had to walk to the black children's school while a bus took the white boys and girls to their school. She later explained that seeing the white children on their bus "was among the first ways I realized there was a black world and a white world."

As an adult, Parks worked as a seamstress. She later explained in her book *Quiet Strength* why she refused to leave her seat on the bus in late 1955: "All I felt was tired. Tired of being pushed around. Tired of seeing the bad treatment of children, women, and men just because of the color of their skin. Tired of the Jim Crow laws. Tired of being oppressed. I was just plain tired."

After the Montgomery Bus Boycott, Mrs. Parks moved to Detroit, Michigan. There she worked many years for John Conyers, an African-American U.S. congressman. "I want to be remembered as a person who stood up to injustice, who wanted a better world for young people," Mrs. Parks writes in *Quiet Strength*. The Mother of the Modern Civil Rights Movement lived to the age of ninety-two.

King of Civil Rights

Martin Luther King Jr. (1929–1968) was born in Atlanta, Georgia. Nicknamed M. L., he was a brilliant student with a beautiful speaking voice and a way with words. King entered Morehouse College when he was only fifteen. Later he became a minister at Montgomery's Dexter Avenue Baptist Church.

In his book *Stride Toward Freedom*, Dr. King provides a close-up view of the Montgomery Bus Boycott. He also expresses his belief in **nonviolent** protest: "We will not hate you, but we cannot in all good conscience obey your unjust laws. Do to us what you will and we will still love you. We will so appeal to your heart and conscience that we will win you in the process."

Dr. King led marches, made speeches, and wrote books about civil rights. In 1963 he gave his famous "I Have a Dream" speech in Washington, D.C. For doing so much to steer the world toward racial equality, he won the 1964 Nobel Peace Prize. The great civil rights leader was shot and killed when he was only thirty-nine years old.

On the afternoon of December 5, Montgomery's African-American leaders gathered at a church to plan their **strategy**. They formed a new organization. At the suggestion of Ralph Abernathy, a young black minister, it was named the Montgomery Improvement Association (MIA). At Edgar Nixon's urging, the organization elected a young minister named Martin Luther King Jr. to serve as its president. Nixon was elected secretary. Reverend Abernathy became vice president.

That Monday night the MIA held a giant meeting at the Holt Street Baptist Church. Six thousand people attended. When a speaker asked if the bus boycott should end after that one day, the crowd shouted, "NO!" Dr. King made a rousing speech. He told the crowd, "We are here to say to those who have mistreated us so long that we are tired of being segregated and humiliated." King cautioned that the protests must remain peaceful, however.

Reverend Abernathy read a **resolution** to the crowd. It was a pledge to continue the boycott until the city took steps to end segregation on its buses. All in favor of the motion were asked to stand. Dr. King later reported that every person in the church stood up.

A college student handles the phone as a car-pool dispatcher during the 1956 bus boycott.

CHAPTER SIX

"For My Children and Grandchildren"

The MIA established a system to help people travel around Montgomery without riding the buses. About 325 people volunteered to serve as drivers. Each morning they picked up passengers who gathered at forty-three "dispatch stations." They drove the passengers to their jobs and schools. Later in the day, the car-pool drivers collected people at forty-two "pickup stations" and took them home.

To make a more visible protest, some people walked. A few walked as many as 12 miles (19 kilometers) to protest segregation on buses. When asked if walking made her tired, one woman said, "I don't mind if my body is tired because my soul is free." Another elderly woman trudged along on

Montgomery's African-American citizens walk to work in protest of the city's segregation laws.

foot and refused a ride by explaining, "I'm not walking for myself. I'm walking for my children and grandchildren."

On Thursday, December 8, Dr. King and other MIA leaders met with city and bus company officials. The officials insisted on keeping the segregated seating system, so the boycott continued. Day after day, nearly all black Montgomerians refused to ride the buses. Some white people joined them in avoiding the buses.

The forces of hatred were strong, however. White **bigots** struck at the boycott's leaders. On the evening of January 30, 1956, while Dr. King was attending an MIA meeting, his house was bombed. Dr. King rushed home. He was relieved to find that his wife, Coretta Scott King, and their infant daughter, Yolanda, were unhurt. Standing on his damaged porch, Dr. King spoke to the hundreds of angry black people who gathered outside his home:

It is regrettable that this has happened, but we must remain peaceful, for we believe in law and order. I did not start this boycott. I was asked by you to serve as your spokesman. I want it known that if I am stopped, this movement will not stop, for what we are doing is right and just! God is with us and is on our side.

Soon afterward, Edgar Nixon's house was bombed. Fortunately he was out of town, and his wife, Arlet, was unharmed. Criminals also bombed the home of Reverend Robert Graetz, a white minister who was prominent in the MIA. No one was inside Graetz's house at the time. Although the violence scared people, it did not stop the boycott. As Arlet Nixon told her husband, "They're trying to make you quit, but don't do it!"

A car-pool driver gets a parking ticket in February 1956.

CHAPTER SEVEN

"Glorious Daybreak": Victory at Last

As the months passed, white authorities tried to break the boycotters' spirit. The Montgomery police gave the car-pool drivers tickets for driving too fast—or too slow. Car-pool driver Jo Ann Robinson later recalled receiving "seventeen traffic tickets for all kinds of trumped-up charges" in early 1956. Authorities also found an old Alabama law forbidding boycotts. In late February more than one hundred boycott leaders, including King, Abernathy, and Mrs. Robinson, were briefly arrested under this law.

The boycott took a heavy toll on the city of Montgomery and the bus company. Each month the city lost about a thousand dollars in **revenue**. The bus company's losses were far greater. In addition, business owners lost

Ralph Abernathy

One of a family of twelve children, Ralph Abernathy (1926–1990) was born in Linden, Alabama. As a young man he worked as a disc jockey at a Montgomery radio station. Later he became a minister. Abernathy and Martin Luther King Jr. were friends. They worked closely to plan and carry out the Montgomery Bus Boycott. During his many years of civil rights work, Abernathy was jailed, and his house and church were bombed. Southern schools, restaurants, theaters, hotels, and buses were desegregated thanks partly to his efforts.

income because African-American shoppers were visiting their stores less frequently. About forty white businessmen formed a new organization called the Men of Montgomery to try to end the boycott. It was composed of "men of good will" according to Dr. King. However, the Men of Montgomery could not settle the dispute because city officials would not budge on the issue of segregation.

The issue was finally settled in court. On February 1, 1956, the MIA filed a suit on behalf of Claudette Colvin, Mary Louise Smith, and three women who had been mistreated on Montgomery's buses. The suit asked that Alabama's and Montgomery's laws segregating people on buses be declared **unconstitutional**. A federal court in Montgomery handed down its decision on June 4, 1956. The court ruled that segregation on Montgomery buses violated the U.S. Constitution's Fourteenth Amendment.

The struggle was not over, though. The city's lawyers appealed the case to the U.S. Supreme Court. Its decision would settle the dispute once and for all. On November 13, 1956, the nation's highest court issued its ruling. The Supreme Court declared that Alabama's state and local laws regarding segregation on buses were unconstitutional.

"This is a glorious daybreak to end a long night of segregation," Dr. King said joyously when he learned of this decision.

The boycott continued for another five weeks until the Supreme Court's order went into effect. On December 21, 1956, segregation on Montgomery's buses finally ended. That day Dr. King, Ralph Abernathy, Edgar Nixon, and Rosa Parks rode on a Montgomery bus. They sat in a section formerly reserved for whites. The yearlong Montgomery Bus Boycott—and segregation on the city's buses—had ended.

African-American leaders, including Dr. King and Ralph Abernathy (next to the windows), ride a Montgomery bus after the victory.

CHAPTER EIGHT

"To Put Justice in Business"

As the boycott ended, Dr. King told an MIA rally, "Our aim has never been to put the bus company out of business, but rather to put justice in business." His words proved true. The Montgomery Bus Boycott was a turning point in the struggle for equality in America. As millions of people watched events unfold on television, the boycott focused attention on the civil rights movement. The successful outcome paved the way for other Southern cities to desegregate their buses.

The boycott also helped spark later civil rights crusades, including such triumphs as the civil rights acts of 1964 and 1968 and the Voting Rights Act of 1965. Moreover, Montgomerians had proved that Dr. King's method of

Crowds fill the mall in Washington, D.C., during the Poor People's March in 1968.

seeking justice by peaceful means worked.

In addition, the boycott showed that the key to winning the civil rights struggle was to work toward a common goal as a group. Following the boycott, African Americans formed organizations such as the Southern Christian Leadership Conference (SCLC) to oppose injustice.

Finally, the boycott brought Martin Luther King Jr. and Ralph Abernathy to the forefront as civil rights leaders. Abernathy later led the 1968 Poor People's March on Washington. He also served as SCLC president. Thanks to the Montgomery Bus Boycott's success, Dr. King began a career as one of the world's foremost champions of civil rights.

Glossary

amendment—An addition or change, especially to a constitution.

bigots—People who dislike others because they are different in some way.

boycott—A refusal to do business with a person, firm, country, or organization in an attempt to receive fairer treatment.

civil rights—Involving people's basic rights and freedoms.

colonies—Settlements built by a country outside its own borders.

constitution—The basic framework of government for a country or state.

customs—Practices that come about by habit rather than by law.

discrimination—The practice of abusing people because of their color, gender, religion, or other characteristic.

immoral—Against what people regard as right or proper.

nonviolent—Peaceful; without violence.

resolution—A proposal, plan, or pledge.

revenue—Money or income.

segregation—The practice of keeping people apart, especially by race.

strategy—A specific way to achieve a goal.

unconstitutional—Violating the basic framework of a nation's government.

Timeline

1780—Massachusetts becomes the first state to outlaw slavery

1860—The North has ended slavery, but there are 4 million slaves in the South

1861—April 12: The Civil War breaks out between the Union (North) and the Confederacy (South)

1865—April 9: The Union wins the Civil War

December 6: The Thirteenth Amendment frees all remaining slaves

1868—The Fourteenth Amendment guarantees African Americans equal rights as citizens

Late 1800s–early 1900s—Jim Crow segregation laws and customs become established throughout the South

1884—Ida B. Wells challenges Tennessee's Jim Crow train-seating law, but ultimately loses her case

1947—Jackie Robinson breaks Major League Baseball's color barrier

1953—Mary Church Terrell's campaign results in a Supreme Court ruling that ends segregation in Washington, D.C., restaurants

1780   *1868*   *1884*

1954—In the *Brown v. Board of Education* case, the Supreme Court rules that segregation in public schools must end

1955—December 1: Following similar efforts by Claudette Colvin and Mary Louise Smith, Rosa Parks challenges Montgomery's Jim Crow bus-seating laws

December 5: The Montgomery Bus Boycott begins

1956—January 30: Dr. King's house is bombed

June 4: A federal court in Montgomery rules that segregation on the city's buses must end

November 13: The U.S. Supreme Court agrees that segregation on buses is unconstitutional

December 21: Segregation on Montgomery buses ends, as does the Montgomery Bus Boycott

1960s—Partly thanks to the Montgomery Bus Boycott, the civil rights acts of 1964 and 1968 and the Voting Rights Act of 1965 are passed

2006—Americans celebrate the fiftieth anniversary of the Montgomery Bus Boycott's victory for justice and equality

1954 *1956* *2006*

Further Information

BOOKS

Collard, Sneed B. III. *Rosa Parks: The Courage to Make a Difference.* New York: Marshall Cavendish Benchmark, 2007.

Freedman, Russell. *Freedom Walkers: The Story of the Montgomery Bus Boycott.* New York: Holiday House, 2006.

Miller, Jake. *The Montgomery Bus Boycott: Integrating Public Buses.* New York: Rosen, 2004.

Schraff, Anne. *Rosa Parks: "Tired of Giving In."* Berkeley Heights, NJ: Enslow, 2005.

WEB SITES

For a wealth of information about the Montgomery Bus Boycott, including biographies of the participants, newspaper articles, photos, videos, and interviews:
http://www.montgomeryboycott.com/frontpage.htm

For an interesting overview of the Montgomery Bus Boycott:
http://www.africanaonline.com/montgomery.htm

For a biography of Rosa Parks:
http://www.rosaparks.org/bio.html

For a biography of Ralph Abernathy:
http://www.notablebiographies.com/A-An/Abernathy-Ralph.html

For a biography of Martin Luther King Jr.:
http://nobelprize.org/nobel_prizes/peace/laureates/1964/king-bio.html

Bibliography

King, Martin Luther Jr. *Stride Toward Freedom: The Montgomery Story.* New York: Harper & Row, 1958.

Parks, Rosa, with Gregory J. Reed. *Quiet Strength: The Faith, the Hope, and the Heart of a Woman Who Changed a Nation.* Grand Rapids, MI: Zondervan Publishing House, 1994.

Robinson, Jo Ann Gibson. *The Montgomery Bus Boycott and the Women Who Started It: The Memoir of Jo Ann Gibson Robinson.* Knoxville: The University of Tennessee Press, 1987.

Williams, Donnie, with Wayne Greenhaw. *The Thunder of Angels: The Montgomery Bus Boycott and the People Who Broke the Back of Jim Crow.* Chicago: Lawrence Hill Books, 2006.

Index

Page numbers in **boldface** are illustrations.

About the Author

Dennis Fradin is the author of 150 books, some of them written with his wife, Judith Bloom Fradin. Their book for Clarion, *The Power of One: Daisy Bates and the Little Rock Nine*, was named a Golden Kite Honor Book. Another of Dennis's well-known books is *Let It Begin Here! Lexington & Concord: First Battles of the American Revolution*, published by Walker. Other recent books by the Fradins include *Jane Addams: Champion of Democracy* for Clarion and *5,000 Miles to Freedom: Ellen and William Craft's Flight from Slavery* for National Geographic Children's Books. Their current project for National Geographic is the *Witness to Disaster* series about natural disasters. *Turning Points in U.S. History* is Dennis's first series for Marshall Cavendish Benchmark. The Fradins have three grown children and five grandchildren.